ONLINE IDENTITY AND PRIVACY
12 THINGS YOU NEED TO KNOW

by Jill Roesler

12 STORY LIBRARY

Camas Public Library

www.12StoryLibrary.com

12-Story Library is an imprint of Peterson Publishing Company and Press Room Editions.

Produced for 12-Story Library by Red Line Editorial

Photographs ©: PeopleImages/iStockphoto, cover, 1; Juergen Faelchle/Shutterstock Images, 4; Monkey Business Images/Shutterstock Images, 5, 18, 19; Digital Vision/Photodisc/ Thinkstock, 6; pogoslaw/iStockphoto/Thinkstock, 7; Di Studio/Shutterstock Images, 8; John Kwan/Shutterstock Images, 9; Fuse/Thinkstock, 10; Jose Luis Pelaez Inc/Blend Images/Thinkstock, 11; Dragon Images/Thinkstock, 12, 29; ConstantinosZ/iStockphoto, 13; scyther5/iStockphoto, 15; Sabphoto/Shutterstock Images, 16; Pixland/Thinkstock, 17; Samuel Borges Photography/Shutterstock Images, 20, 28; bikeriderlondon/Shutterstock Images, 21; FotoMaximum/iStockphoto/Thinkstock, 22; Mark Van Scyoc/Shutterstock Images, 23; GaudiLab/Shutterstock Images, 25; AAraujo/Shutterstock Images, 26; shironosov/iStockphoto/Thinkstock, 27

ISBN
978-1-63235-221-7 (hardcover)
978-1-63235-247-7 (paperback)
978-1-62143-272-2 (hosted ebook)

Library of Congress Control Number: 2015934327

Printed in the United States of America
Mankato, MN
October, 2015

Go beyond the book. Get free, up-to-date content on this topic at 12StoryLibrary.com.

TABLE OF CONTENTS

WHAT IS AN ONLINE IDENTITY?

Lots of characteristics make up your identity. Your likes, dislikes, personality, and even your physical appearance make you unique. Your online identity works the same way, just online.

When you visit websites, they learn a little bit about you. These little bits are used to create your online identity. Each website you visit will see your characteristics differently. These characteristics are called partial identities. Imagine you buy a pair of shoes online. The website will remember your shoe size. Your shoe size is a partial identity. The website stores the information to create a partial identity for you. Other websites may

Your identity is made up of the things that make you unique.

77

Percent of Internet users who read blogs.

- Everyone who uses the Internet has a unique online identity.
- Websites create partial identities for their users.
- You do not decide how a website identifies you, but you do decide what information is part of your persona.

collect the information and use it. You might not know when a website creates a partial identity for you.

THINK ABOUT IT

What does your online identity say about the real you? Make a list of the partial identities you think you have. How are they similar to parts of your real identity? How are they different?

Your persona is a partial identity you create. When you write on a blog or post a video to a social network, you develop your persona online. You decide what information is part of your persona. It may not be the same as your personality offline.

What you post online helps make up your online identity.

5

CAN MY ONLINE IDENTITY DIFFER FROM MY REAL ONE?

The way a person describes him or herself is different for everyone. Some people describe themselves as shy. Others say they are outgoing. Both of these characteristics describe how people relate to others.

The interactions people have with parents, teachers, and friends help them decide how to describe themselves. Imagine a boy describes himself as shy. He bases his description on how he acts around others. Now imagine he is chatting with an online friend. The online friend probably wouldn't know the boy is shy.

It's important to always be yourself, whether in real life or online. But online, you can choose how much

Someone who is shy in real life may be outgoing online.

GEORGE HERBERT MEAD

George Herbert Mead was a scientist during the late 1800s and early 1900s. He studied psychology and sociology. His work says people's personalities are shaped by the time they spend with others. The way people think about themselves is a reflection of what others think of them.

of yourself you want to share. Some people choose to show only certain aspects of their personalities online. A person who is shy in real life may be more outgoing online. Online, people have the chance to be a little different than they are in real life. But online social interactions are quite different from personal ones. You cannot hear voices or see gestures or facial expressions. It can be difficult to understand how another person is feeling.

1
Number of young people, out of three, who say they feel more accepted online than in real life.

- The interactions you have with others help determine the traits that contribute to your identity.
- Today, most people have two different identities: a real-life identity and an online identity.
- Having real-world interactions helps you better understand yourself.

Interpreting someone's emotions online is more difficult than in real life.

HOW DO I PROTECT MY PRIVATE INFORMATION?

Many websites gather your personal information to sell you products. Some websites ask users to make an account before viewing certain webpages. Some of the information a website requests is optional to fill out. You decide whether or not to share it. If information is optional, limit what you share.

There are two basic kinds of information to share online: personal information and private information. Personal information includes facts about you, such as your age and your favorite food. It cannot be used to identify you as an individual. Private information, though, can identify you. It can include your name, home address, and e-mail address. Personal information is safer to share than private information. But it can be easy to share private information when you share personal information. You might share that you like the pizza your school serves. This is personal

Username

Password

Log in

Be careful with your private information when you create accounts online.

information. But the name and location of your school is private information. You might accidentally share it when you share how much you like the pizza. It is important to think before you share your personal information online. It is even more important to think before you share private information.

If you share too much private information, there is a chance someone could steal your identity. Identity theft happens when someone uses private information to pretend to be somebody else. Thieves steal other people's Social Security numbers, birth dates, or credit card numbers. They use the data to get identification cards or credit cards illegally. Identity thieves are difficult to catch. Many of them do not think about how their actions affect real people.

14

Percent of all consumer complaints the government received in 2013 that were about identity theft.

- Some of the information you give to websites is optional to share.
- Personal information and private information are the two basic types of information people share online.
- An identity thief steals another person's Social Security number, birth date, or credit card information.

Keep your Social Security number private to avoid identity theft.

WHEN IS MY PERSONAL INFORMATION COLLECTED ONLINE?

Websites collect your personal information and sell it to advertising companies.

Companies use parts of your identity to make money. They collect your personal information to create targeted advertisements. They might use the websites you visit, your interests, your birthday, and your ZIP code. You decide whether or not to provide companies with your personal information.

Websites collect your personal information when you create an account. In the process, you may give websites permission to gather

SHARE WITH CARE

You can limit how much information websites collect about you. One way is to be aware of what you share online. Keep your address, phone number, and location private. Ask an adult before you post pictures of yourself online.

COPPA limits the information websites may collect from kids.

your personal information. This permission is found in websites' terms and conditions. These are the

12
Maximum age of the children COPPA protects.

- Websites use people's personal information to create targeted advertisements.
- People want to control what kind of information they share online.
- A website's terms and conditions often give the website permission to use your personal data.

rules you agree to when you create an account. It is unlikely a company will contact you directly. But once you give information away, there is no way to get it back. You may not be able to ask a company to remove it.

Most Americans are surprised by the amount of personal information companies collect. Some people want to be able to control how much information they provide. In 1998, Congress passed a new law. It was called the Children's Online Privacy Protection Act, or COPPA. It limits the information websites may collect from children. It helps protect children's online privacy.

HOW DO WEB BROWSERS USE COOKIES?

Your web browser stores a cookie from each website you visit. A cookie is a strand of information. It is made up of little bits of data you leave behind on a site. Websites place cookies in your browser's folder. When you go back to the site later, it uses the cookies to remember you. That is how your information and preferences appear each time you go back to a website. The cookie remembers your personal data so using the site is easier.

A different kind of cookie accesses personal information other cookies contain. It is called a third-party cookie. Third-party cookies share your information with other websites. These sites use your data to make a profit.

Websites use cookies to track the pages you visit.

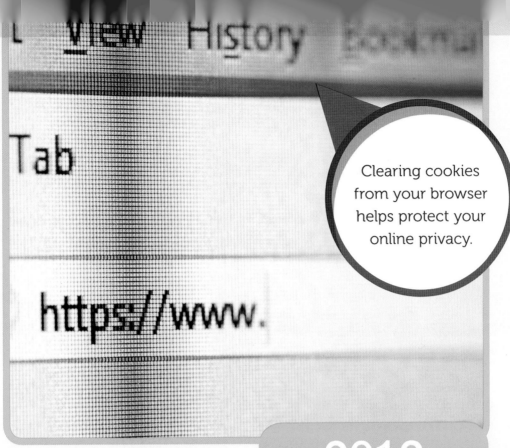

Clearing cookies from your browser helps protect your online privacy.

You can delete cookies from your browser. An adult can show you how. But some websites will not function without them. So it is important to think about what information you share. Imagine writing in a friend's yearbook with a pen. You can try to cover up what you wrote. But it is still there, under the surface. It cannot be erased. It is better to think about what you write first.

2012
Year Verizon began using difficult-to-erase supercookies to track its 106 million retail customers.

- Your preferences for each website you visit are saved using a cookie.
- Companies use cookies to make using websites easier.
- It is important to think about what you share online before you do so.

WHY SHOULD I CHANGE MY PASSWORDS?

To make an account on a website, you will be asked to create a password. Passwords help make sure no one else sees your personal and private information. Strong passwords help protect your online identity. They keep your information private.

THINK ABOUT IT

Experts recommend changing your passwords every six months. What are some reasons you might need to change your passwords sooner?

With a pencil, write down five practice passwords using the tips in this book. Once you are finished, make sure to erase them in case you want to use one in the future.

Many Internet users reuse the same password for each web account they own. Others may use similar passwords. But online privacy experts suggest using a different password for each account. Hackers can easily figure out common passwords because many include personal information. People often use birthdays, a last name, or the name of a relative in passwords. This information can be easy for hackers to learn.

Strong passwords use a combination of letters, numbers, and symbols. The strongest contain at least six characters. A character is a letter, number, or symbol. Trustworthy passwords use a combination of lowercase letters, uppercase letters, numbers, or symbols. Think of a phrase or a quote that you can easily remember. Use the first letter

Hackers try to steal your private information.

of each word in the quote to make an acronym. Imagine your phrase is "I want to protect my online privacy forever." Your acronym could be "Iwtpmop4e." Do your best to change your passwords every six months.

Memorize your passwords. Never keep written copies of your passwords, especially someplace near a computer. Instead, use a password manager. Password management websites securely store and keep track of passwords. Only share your passwords with a trusted adult. Do not give your friends or people you meet online your passwords. Protecting your passwords helps protect your online identity.

127

Maximum number of characters a Microsoft password can contain.

- Use a different password for each of your online accounts.
- A strong password contains at least six characters.
- Only share your passwords with a trusted adult.

HOW DO I SPOT AN ONLINE PREDATOR?

The Internet offers valuable information. But some online content is not appropriate for children and teenagers. There are few laws that control what is published on the Internet. Anyone can build a website for any reason.

Some sites allow people to buy and sell stolen and illegal goods. The sale of the goods is illegal. But creating the website is not. There are also websites that support harmful things such as drug use. An Internet search can lead you to offensive material. It is important that you know what you are looking for online. Having a plan can help you avoid offensive content.

People you meet online are not always who they say they are.

There are ways you can spot an online predator. One sign is if someone will talk over the phone but never over a webcam. A predator might send gifts, photos, or letters before asking to meet in person.

It can be difficult to know if you are talking to a predator, so be alert. Tell an adult if you suspect something unusual about a person you met over chat. Do not video chat with someone you do not know in real life. It's all part of being a smart Internet user.

Don't use webcams with people you don't know in real life.

It is especially important to be careful when using online chat. Chats make communication easier. But you never truly know who is on the other end of the conversation. It is common for predatory offenders to use chat. They pretend to be children or teenagers. They talk about things that interest children or teens. Eventually, predators earn a child's trust. This trust could lead to meeting face to face. This could put the victim in a dangerous situation.

75
Percent of Internet crimes between predators and children that go unreported.

- There are few laws regulating the Internet.
- An Internet search can bring up offensive material in the results.
- Online chat is the most likely place to encounter a predatory offender.

WHY DO ADULTS WATCH WHAT I DO ONLINE?

Sometimes it feels like your parents or teachers watch your online activity too much. They might ask questions about your online activity. They may want to know the passwords to your online accounts. It can feel like they are invading your privacy.

Most of the time, though, that is not the case. Trusted adults look out for your safety. They want to help protect your online identity.

Parents often set up the family computer in a common area of the

Sometimes it feels like adults are spying on your online activity.

Adults need to know they can trust your judgment when you're online.

house. This way, they can watch your activity from afar. When an adult sees you using the Internet responsibly, they can better trust your judgment. You can explore the Internet together. You can also teach them about your interests.

It is okay to ask questions about the websites you are curious about. Asking questions helps you use the Internet responsibly. Try asking a parent, an older sibling, a trusted adult, or a teacher. Learning about online dangers now will help you become a responsible Internet user.

13

Age most adults think children should be before using the Internet on their own.

- Trusted adults who monitor your Internet use are looking out for your safety.
- When an adult sees that you can use the Internet responsibly, he or she is more likely to trust your judgment.
- It is okay to ask questions about the websites you are curious about.

CAN I DELETE THINGS I WRITE AND UPLOAD ONLINE?

The information you put online builds your online identity. So does the information others post about you. But sometimes, you post something you may later regret. Someone else could also post offensive material about you without your permission.

You can usually hide the content you add to a website. But that information often remains on the website. It is never permanently deleted. Look through the comment section of a website. You might see a post that says "deleted comment." The words are no longer visible. But the spot for that comment still exists. People with knowledge of how the Internet works can still retrieve that information. Most people will not try to retrieve a deleted comment, but some might.

Be careful about what you choose to post online.

Deleting content directly from a website is the best and simplest way to remove minor mistakes. But sometimes you need to delete something more private. You can contact the website's webmaster and ask them for help. Webmasters help websites run smoothly. They also control the content of a website. Webmasters decide whether to remove unwanted material.

Mistakes happen. But the Internet is not very forgiving. It can be very tricky to reverse a mistake. That is why it is crucial to think through the potential consequences of uploading certain material. If you are asking yourself if you should share content, it is better to not share it.

Think before you post or share anything online.

THINK ABOUT IT

Have you ever wished you could take back something you posted online? What did you do when it happened? Make a list of the steps you would take if you accidentally posted something online.

22

Percent of youth who admit they use a mobile device to hide online behavior from their parents.

- Online content is never permanently deleted.
- A webmaster ensures that a website is running smoothly and controls its content.
- It is very important to think through the potential consequences of sharing information online.

21

HOW CAN I PROTECT MY PRIVACY ONLINE?

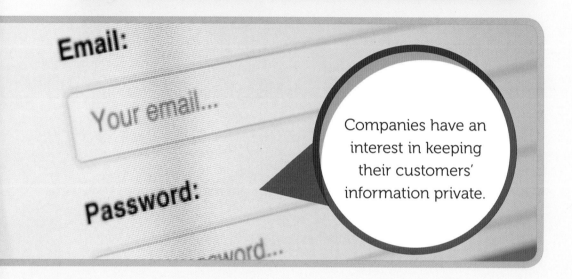

Companies have an interest in keeping their customers' information private.

Researchers believe that as technology advances, people will gain more control over their privacy. People want to have their online privacy protected. They will demand websites protect their private information. If not, they may take their business elsewhere. Eventually, websites will want to protect their customers from unwanted invasions of privacy.

But as online companies add more privacy controls, those that track information will create stronger cookies. Many websites now use supercookies. Supercookies are cookies designed to be permanently stored on a user's computer. You can turn off normal cookies by selecting the "Do Not Track" option in your web browser. But supercookies bypass the "Do Not Track" setting. They continue to track your online movement. They

WHO GOVERNS THE INTERNET?

The Internet was made available to the public in 1991. The US Federal Communications Commission (FCC) had trouble figuring out how to regulate it. The web is a global network. The FCC is a US government agency. It does not have control over websites in other countries.

can also track your activity if your browser is set to private.

Experts claim the public's desire for privacy will eventually win over supercookies. Some say, eventually, you may be able to trade your information with companies. In return, they would provide a service to you. But no one can actually see into the future. The best way to protect the future of your privacy is to look out for its well-being today.

29

Number of months Verizon used supercookies to track customers without giving them a choice to opt out.

- People express more concern now about privacy issues than in the past.
- Supercookies bypass your browser's privacy settings to continue tracking online activity.
- Experts predict people will be able to trade their personal information with companies in return for products and services.

The FCC has had a hard time regulating the Internet.

FEDERAL COMMUNICATIONS COMMISSION

WHAT CAN I DO TO PROTECT MYSELF ONLINE?

Keeping your online identity private can also keep you safe in real life. Secure your online accounts with strong passwords and security questions. Remember to share this information only with a trusted adult. If you've shared it with others, change your passwords to keep your online identity safe. Sometimes, changing your password may not be enough. You may need to contact a website's webmaster. He or she can shut down your account. Then you can open a new one with a new password.

Adjust the privacy settings on any new online account you create. Use them to control who is able to see what you post. Be smart about what you post on social media sites. The best way to protect your privacy is to not share private or personal information. Think twice before you post. Do not

share when your family goes on vacation. Thieves often look on social media to learn when families will be out of town. Remember that nothing gets deleted online. If you would not want a grandparent to read your post, do not share it.

55

Percent of Internet users who have tried to hide from specific people or organizations online.

- Protecting your identity online helps you stay safe in real life.
- Create strong passwords to protect your private and personal information.
- Be careful about what you post to social media.

24

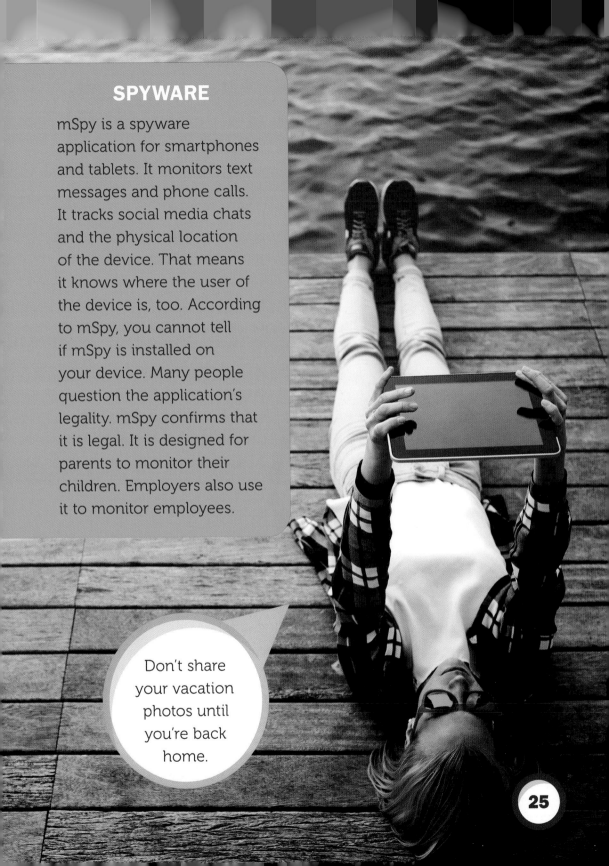

SPYWARE

mSpy is a spyware application for smartphones and tablets. It monitors text messages and phone calls. It tracks social media chats and the physical location of the device. That means it knows where the user of the device is, too. According to mSpy, you cannot tell if mSpy is installed on your device. Many people question the application's legality. mSpy confirms that it is legal. It is designed for parents to monitor their children. Employers also use it to monitor employees.

Don't share your vacation photos until you're back home.

HOW CAN MY ONLINE IDENTITY HELP ME?

Your online identity and the way you use the Internet can be helpful. Over time, your online identity could contribute to who you are in real life. If you exercise a healthy curiosity online, you might discover more in real life.

Students benefit greatly from using the Internet. Not only is it an educational tool, it can also show you how the world works. Museums let you take virtual tours. It is like taking a field trip from school or home. Some online tours let you swim with whales, visit ancient ruins, or even walk on the moon. Exploring the web can be an excellent way to learn.

When you use the Internet safely, you can learn lots of new things. When you share what you've learned with

The Internet makes it possible to visit faraway places from your home.

friends and family online, it creates a positive online identity. Instead of sharing private information, you're sharing knowledge. You can take this knowledge with you in real life. It helps make you who you are. Using the Internet safely helps you build a positive identity online and in real life, too.

Share knowledge online rather than personal information.

66

Percent of Internet users who have images of themselves posted online.

- The Internet can help you create a positive online identity.
- Your positive online identity helps create a positive real-life identity.
- Using the web in a safe way will contribute to a positive online identity.

CELEBRATE YOUR SUCCESS

Use the Internet to document your accomplishments. Share photos of yourself winning an award or sliding into home plate. This type of sharing contributes to a positive online identity. Celebrate your success online and let others share your excitement! Remember not to compare yourself with others. Most people share only positive things about themselves. Congratulate them instead of competing with them.

FACT SHEET

- Most social media websites let you report inappropriate comments. Reporting this information is called flagging. Flagging inappropriate comments keeps social media sites safe. It makes sure your private information stays private. It helps prevent people from getting hurt.

- Cyberbullies use different kinds of technology to pick on other people. The bully might use social media, e-mail, mobile apps, or websites to spread rumors or say hurtful things. They might share private information about others. Being the victim of a cyberbully is not your fault. But it is your job to report cyberbullying if it happens to you or if you see it happen to others.

- A "catfish" is someone who pretends to be another person, real or fake, in order to fool someone online. Usually, the catfish wants the other person to fall in love with him or her. They do so by posting fake photos and false information on a social media website. Be careful about adding friends you do not know on social media websites. You never know who could be catfishing you.

- The Children's Internet Protection Act (CIPA) helps you avoid offensive content at school. Schools receive discounts on their Internet access if they block inappropriate content online. CIPA requires schools to teach students how to use the Internet safely and protect their online identities.

GLOSSARY

cookie
A small amount of data generated by a website and saved by your web browser.

hacker
A person who illegally accesses another person's computer system.

online identity
An identity an Internet user creates by using websites and participating in online communities.

partial identity
A portion of the characteristics that make up an online identity.

persona
A partial identity you create to represent yourself in a specific situation.

personal information
Facts about yourself that could apply to many other people.

private information
Particular facts about yourself you should not share with anyone.

spyware
Software that gathers information about an Internet user.

targeted advertisement
A promotion intended to reach a specific audience.

web browser
An application, such as Google Chrome or Internet Explorer, used to access and view websites.

webmaster
The person who maintains the content and operation of a website.

FOR MORE INFORMATION

Books

Jakubiak, David J. *A Smart Kid's Guide to Internet Privacy*. New York: PowerKids Press, 2010.

Mason, Paul. *Understanding Computer Safety*. Chicago: Heinemann Library, 2015.

Morretta, Alison. *How to Maintain Your Privacy Online*. New York: Cavendish Square, 2015.

Websites

How Cyber-Savvy Are You?: Media Smarts
www.mediasmarts.ca/sites/mediasmarts/files/games/cyber-security-quiz/index_en.html

KidsHealth: Internet Safety
www.kidshealth.org/parent/positive/family/net_safety.html

PBS Kids: Webonauts Internet Academy
www.pbskids.org/webonauts

INDEX

About the Author

Jill Roesler was a professional journalist before she began writing children's books. She enjoys doing research and writing about historical topics, as well as modern-day society. Jill is from Minnesota.

READ MORE FROM 12-STORY LIBRARY

Every 12-Story Library book is available in many formats, including Amazon Kindle and Apple iBooks. For more information, visit your device's store or 12StoryLibrary.com.